DRAWING A CAT

DRAWING A CAT

BY CLARE TURLAY NEWBERRY

With an Introduction
by Thomas Craven

THE STUDIO: NEW YORK & LONDON

To Jennie Wasson
with Love

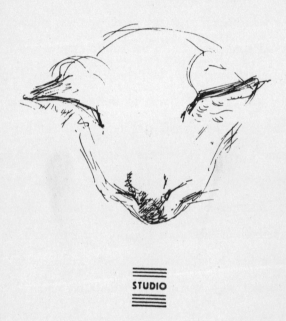

STUDIO

Printed in U.S.A. by The New York Lithographing Co., and published in New York by The Studio Publications, Inc., 381 Fourth Avenue, in London by The Studio Limited, 66 Chandos Place.

INTRODUCTION

Clare Turlay Newberry has been singularly fortunate as an artist. At the very beginning of her career she was attached, by natural and unforced interests, to the subject-matter which she has made peculiarly her own; at the age when most painters blindly follow the formal regimen of the studio, she was an advanced student of the animal kingdom, certain of her aims and her talents. As a consequence, instead of imposing a borrowed or extraneous technique upon her subjects, she has developed by sustained observation and affectionate enthusiasm her special method, or individual style, of rendering cats. In all her work, from her swift pencil notations to her most finished studies in line and wash, she displays remarkable understanding of the spirit of cats : their self-absorption, their secrecy and impulsiveness, their indignation and furtive petulancies—all the moods and tempers of these sly, undomesticated companions.

For cats, as she will tell you, are wary and entrancing things—

easy to reduce to clever designs and easier still to efface in soft outlines and shapeless bundles of fur, but difficult in the extreme to represent with a draughtsmanship revealing the subtleties of muscular action and rhythmical attitudes without destroying the essential character of the animal. Clare Newberry has triumphed over the difficulties, and more. With a technique perfectly adapted to her subjects—a method which appears to be the simplest and most spontaneous style in the world, until one has tried it—she seizes on and preserves not only the postures and muscular action but the charm, the playfulness, and most important, the personality of cats. In short, her insight into cat-life and her knowledge of structure, together with her skill as a draughtsman and her extraordinary lightness of touch, have enabled her to delineate the little inhabitants of her chosen kingdom in the engaging attitudes and with the personal distinction usually reserved by artists for human beings.

THOMAS CRAVEN

DRAWING A CAT

Cats do *not* pose for the artist, and except when asleep seldom

stay in one position for more than a few moments. In order to

Pen sketch of "Babette."

Brush drawing from life of "Nicolett

learn to draw them you must make hundreds of quick sketches

from life.   What appears on your sketch pad in the early stages

Pen sketch of "Boojum."

Sketch of "Babette" and "Boojum."

of studying a cat does not matter. What does matter is the

intense, concentrated observation that accompanies the act of

drawing. Every moment of this kind of observation will add to

your knowledge of the animal, until eventually you will have a

store of visual impressions which you will use instinctively when drawing cats either from memory or from life.

I never try to make a finished picture of a cat until I have

studied it for two or three weeks at least. I begin by making a

great many rapid sketches. And at this stage I am careful to

draw only what I see, stopping a sketch the instant the cat moves,

"Black Persian Cat."

instead of finishing from memory as I am tempted to do. Other-

wise my studies might be misleading to me later, when I had

forgotten where observation left off and guess-work began.

Below : Conte crayon drawing from life of "Nip" who
belonged to the late Constance Lindsay Skinner for nearly
eighteen years. This was a study for a pastel portrait.

Conte crayon sketches
of "Boojum" on
newsprint paper.

Black chalk sketch of "Danny."

I never use an eraser when sketching. My object is to saturate my mind with visual images of the model, and any fussiness about what appears on the paper would destroy my concentration and defeat my purpose.

Below : Pen sketch of "Blue Boy of Stonehedge," a pedigreed Siamese, done when I had been studying cats for only a few months. "Blue Boy" was my first cat model, and my favourite of all the cats I have ever known.

Opposite : "Negro" pencil drawing from life of "Wimpy." This is almost only detailed cat drawing I have ever been able to do entirely from life. "Wimpy" held this pose for at least half an hour. He was a rather torpid cat.

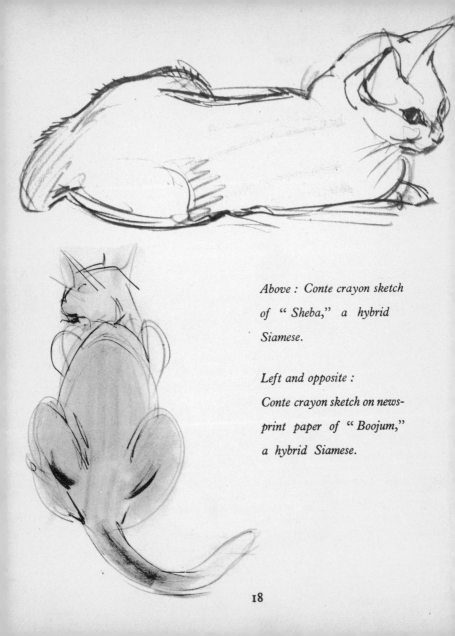

Above : Conte crayon sketch of " Sheba," a hybrid Siamese.

Left and opposite : Conte crayon sketch on news-print paper of " Boojum," a hybrid Siamese.

"Boojum," as opposite.

This method of working is very different from that used in a

" life " class, where one draws in a leisurely fashion for perhaps

twenty minutes, and then rests for five or ten. I don't allow

myself rest periods while sketching, but work steadily for an hour

or two at a time, starting a new sketch each time the cat moves.

This is a very exhausting process and I usually want to quit before I have been at it long. If, however, I can force myself to continue past the fatigue point, I find my second wind and forget about being tired. Gradually my speed and accuracy increase, along with the intensity of my concentration, until I am drawing with the most furious rapidity. This stage lasts only a few minutes—half-an-hour at most—but it is then that I do my best drawing.

Although a cat may hold still long enough for you to catch the entire pose it can be assumed that he will never give you time to finish the details, such as eyes, ears, nostrils, and whiskers.

Two studies of "Babette," the Siamese kitten.
(Courtesy Harper & Bros., New York.)

Six Sk
(from life,

"Mittens"
("egro" pencil).

These must all be studied minutely, one by one, until you can

draw them from memory from any angle.

In order to stimulate my interest and get as much work out

of myself as possible, I often change my medium during a sketch

"Saroyan," a Siamese Cat.

*Studies of a Tabby Cat and a
Siamese Cat and Kitten.*

End papers for "Mittens" (New York, Harper. London, Hamish Hamilton). This was one of the most difficult things

I ever did, for each end paper was done in one sheet of wet paper which meant that I had to work on five kittens at the same time.

period.   Sometimes in the course of one day's work I may use

charcoal, Conte crayon, pen-and-ink, and lead pencil.

Occasionally, when I can't make myself draw at all, I simply

stare fixedly at the cat for half an hour or so, drawing it mentally

and deliberately memorizing certain details about the markings,

"Negro" pencil sketch of "Edward."

"Negro" pencil sketch of "Edward."

proportions, colours, direction of growth of fur, and so on.

Cats are hard enough to draw, but kittens are a great deal harder. Their bodies are softer and less well-defined than that of a grown cat, they are much livelier, and they grow so fast that there is little opportunity for the prolonged study one can give an adult animal.

Mittens, hero of my book of that name, was the first young

kitten I had ever tried to draw, although I had been studying

cats for nearly two years when I began on him.   Being used to

Conte crayon sketch of "Edward."

Black chalk sketch of "Danny"

33

Brush drawing of "Wimpy."

drawing grown cats, I at first found difficulty in getting the very different proportions of a young kitten, especially as these proportions were changing daily. And what I wanted most of all to catch—his pathetic baby look—was gone almost before I knew it. Even his colour scheme changed in the course of a week or two, for the pure white circles around his eyes darkened to a light

Sketch of "Mittens."

brown, destroying the brilliant dark-light contrast which had

been so beautiful.

Pencil Sketches of "Babette."

*Pencil Sketches
of "Babette."*

37

I took Mittens at the age of four weeks and drew him daily for

about a month.   He had already outgrown his baby looks before

the end of that time, and the difference in his appearance was

beginning to conflict with my memory of him as he was at six weeks, the age I wanted to portray. So I stopped drawing him

from life and began on the book illustrations, working partly

from studies and partly from memory. To get the effect of fur

Pen sketches of "Babette."

"Edward" from my book "Barkis" (Harper, New York, Hamish Hamilton, London).

I used charcoal grey water colour on wet paper, adding details

Pencil sketches of "Mittens."

Pencil sketches of "Wimpy."

with crayon when the paper had dried.   I had used a wet paper

technique before, but it was not until I began working on the

Pencil sketch of "Babette."

*Miscellaneous Pen sketches of
"Babette" and "Mittens."*

45

Below is another pencil sketch of "Mittens," drawn on an ordinary piece of soft drawing paper. Opposite, Black chalk sketches of "Danny."

Black chalk sketches of "Danny."

47

Blue Point Siamese ca

"Mittens" illustrations that I achieved the furry effect and the rich blacks I was trying to get. It took me about four months to execute this set of illustrations.

Pencil sketch of "Blue Toyanna of Stonehedge," the mother of "Babette."

Heads of "Babette" at the age of two days.

I began drawing Babette, the Siamese kitten of my second cat

book, the day after her birth. Thus I was able to study her for

about two months before she outgrew her usefulness as a kitten

model. A Siamese cat is born white and the dark " points "

Crayon sketch of
   "Saroyan."

Brush drawing of "Danny."

Clare Turlo, Neule

develop slowly, beginning a day or so after birth.   At first there

is only the faintest smudge of brown or grey on the nose, around

the edge of the ears, and on the paws and tail.   These " points " develop gradually into the dark mask, paws, and tail of the adult

Siamese. Babette was a " blue-point " Siamese, which means

that her " points " were grey instead of the more familiar dark

brown of a " seal-point." In the book " Babette," however, I

gave her " seal-point " markings in order to make the illustrations

bolder and more effective.

My illustrations in this technique are drawn with a brush

directly on wet paper, an operation that takes perhaps five

Pencil sketch of "Babette."

Sketch of "Mittens."

"Babette."

"Charcoal" (from "April's Kittens,"
Harper & Bros.)

minutes. The catch in it lies in the fact that I must usually spoil

thirty or forty pictures before I get one that is good enough to

use. In this, as in sketching from life, my best results are apt

to come at the end of an hour or two of work. As I do the same

drawing over and over my timing of the brush strokes—so

important in a wet paper technique—becomes almost automatic.

I draw more boldly and decoratively, simplifying the design with

each repetition, and no longer thinking of the drawing as a

representation of a cat, but rather as a problem in abstract design.

And I keep on doing this until eventually, by a sort of miracle, I

manage to get the effect I want.

This is, if possible, an even more nerve-wracking process than that of sketching the cat from life, and I have tried many times to discover a short-cut to the effect I want, always without success. The obvious way would be to draw the picture in pencil first and paint over it, but when I try this I find that in

Conte crayon sketch of "Sheba."

Conte crayon sketch of "Danny."

"Babette."

following the guide lines my brush stroke is slowed down and

weakened.   The whole drawing at once becomes less alive.   So

I always go back to the direct method, maddening though it is.